Chinese New Year

Heather C. Hudak

Weigl

Published by Weigl Educational Publishers Limited
6325 10 Street S.E.
Calgary, Alberta
T2H 2Z9

www.weigl.com

Library and Archives Canada Cataloguing in Publication data available upon request.
Fax 403-233-7769 for the attention of the Publishing Records department.

ISBN 978-1-55388-522-1 (hard cover)
ISBN 978-1-55388-527-6 (soft cover)

Printed in the United States of America
1 2 3 4 5 6 7 8 9 0 13 12 11 10 09

Editor: Heather C. Hudak
Design: Terry Paulhus

Every reasonable effort has been made to trace ownership and to obtain permission to reprint copyright material. The
publishers would be pleased to have any errors or omissions brought to their attention so that they may be corrected
in subsequent printings.

Weigl acknowledges Getty Images as one of its primary image suppliers for this title.

We gratefully acknowledge the financial support of the Government of Canada through the Book Publishing Industry
Development Program (BPIDP) for our publishing activities.

Contents

What is Chinese New Year?

One of the most important Chinese holidays is Chinese New Year. It is so important that there are 15 days of celebrations.

The Chinese Calendar

Chinese New Year starts on the first day of the first month of the Chinese calendar. The dates on a Chinese calendar are decided by the position of the Sun and the Moon in the sky. The New Year falls between January and February, but the exact date changes each year.

Sweeping out Evil

To prepare for the New Year, people clean their homes. Tradition says that they should use brooms to sweep out bad luck from the past year. Brooms are put away on the first day of the New Year so good luck cannot be swept out.

A Fresh Start

As the New Year draws near, many people buy new clothes and get a haircut. This gives them a fresh start.

10

The Colour Red

New Year's clothes and decorations often are red. Red is thought to prevent bad luck. The Chinese also believe the colour red scares away evil spirits.

Family Fun

Celebrations begin on New Year's Eve. Families often eat a large dinner together on this special night. Fish is a main part of this meal. Seafood is a symbol of luck, wealth, and happiness. After dinner, families play games until **midnight**. Then, there are fireworks.

15

Special Visits

The first day of Chinese New Year is a time to visit with parents, grandparents, and other family. Married couples give children red **envelopes** filled with money. Then, families go door-to-door greeting their neighbours.

Small Gifts

While visiting friends and family during the New Year, people give small gifts to others. Most gifts are food, such as cookies, fruit, cake, or candy.

Paper Lanterns

The **Lantern** Festival happens on the last day of Chinese New Year. Children carry paper lanterns to **temples** at night. They try to solve riddles that are written on the lanterns.

20

21

Dressing Like Dragons

The dragon is an important part of New Year's celebrations. It is a symbol of strength, goodness, and good luck. People often dress like dragons for New Year's parades.

Glossary

| envelopes | lantern |
| midnight | temples |

Index